WELCOME TO
MEMORY LANE

VOL. 3

RICHMOND, VA

Presented by

K L E O S
INTERNATIONAL, INC.

8400 Meadowbridge Road
Mechanicsville, VA 23116
phone (804) 221-0875
www.kleosmagazine.com

"Memory Lane, Richmond, VA – Vol. 3"
ISBN-13: 978-1-928662-98-3

Design and Layout by Landis Productions LLC

Printed by Lewis Creative Technologies

Written by R. David Ross

Edited by Steven T. Martinenza

Dedicated to Dolores M. Ross

A portion of the proceeds of this book
is being donated to
children's charities throughout the region.

Introduction

The initial two volumes of Memory Lane of Richmond were truly a joy to compile. Even more enjoyment has come out of talking to so many of you about your recollections, reading your letters and emails, and speaking to many community and civic groups about your happy times in the Richmond of old. From senior communities to church groups to women's clubs, I have had the most pleasurable honor to meet and speak with thousands of Richmonders with so many unique and heartfelt memories to share. And of course, whenever a memory is discussed, another emerges...thus, the creation of Volume Three. Please keep your thoughts coming and join me once again as we walk down Memory Lane.

– R. David Ross

Table of Contents

A supper club? In Richmond?

For over two years, it was talked about as being *the* entertainment venue for the area. It would bring top-notch bands and other entertainment to Richmonders. A club-like setting with over-the-top contemporary décor would serve as a site for gatherings, parties, nights-on-the-town and would give Richmond the feel of a much bigger city. What was this much-discussed place going to be? Richmond's **2001 Supper Club.** Located in the West End, 2001 was a membership club where $40 got you on the so-called "elite" list of members. Dionne Warwick headlined the grand opening. Huey Lewis and the News played there shortly after. Though it was operated for a couple of years, the idea and concept never really caught on. If you went once, you saw enough to keep you from going back.

We thought we were getting "night life at its finest." Apparently, Richmonders wanted something more…or maybe something less.

Strike? Spare? Gutter ball?

If you lived north of the river and had a hankering to go bowling, there was no question where you went – **Azalea Bowl.** On the same property as Azalea Mall, the bowling alley was located on the north side of the lot, across from Woolco. Leagues met there daily. Birthday Bowling Parties were held there for adults and children alike. As kids, bowling was also viewed as a "family-style outing." Rent your shoes and pay for the lanes. Grab your hot dogs and drinks and a Saturday would fly by.

With the advent of so many different types of entertainment, games, and video technologies, business waned and Azalea Bowl closed. The building was razed by the developers that purchased the property. Decades later, the entire property still sits empty.

The days of hats, gloves, suits and other finery

Need new gloves and a hat for the Tea Room? A new suit for dancing at Tantilla? A party dress for a family function? One of the first places you would stop was **Berry-Burk.** A longtime upscale men's and women's clothing retailer, Berry-Burk served generations of Richmond families. Originally opened as a dry goods store in 1879, it moved to 6th and Grace Streets in 1926 and officially became Berry-Burk in 1931. The architecture on the outside of the building was known as being as intricate and desirable as the clothing on the inside.

With the expansion of suburban megamalls and major retailers, Berry-Burk Clothing closed in 1989. The Renaissance Revival building has been richly preserved and restored. It is now the location of some of Richmond's finest downtown luxury living.

Household goods? Toys? Appliances? Gasoline?

If we needed just about anything for the home or automobile, we knew we could find it at a Richmond-based store called **Carousel.** The biggest and most often-shopped was located at West Broad Street and Dickens Road in Richmond's West End. It was best known as a "one-stop" discount department store for all things useful. Carousel was purchased by Ward's TV, founded, owned and operated by the Wurtzel family. As Ward's moved toward a superstore concept, it ultimately sold off the Carousel Company, as well as another Richmond mainstay, "Sight 'N Sound" stores. Though this streamlining allowed Ward's to refocus its mission and ultimately become a national powerhouse in the electronics industry with the development of Circuit City, the loss of Carousel was felt for quite some time. Similar stores such as Zayre's were dying out and the Wal-Marts of the world had yet to even enter the market.

Burlington Coat Factory is now at the former Carousel location. An all clothing store, it doesn't have the many uses we remember of Carousel.

Finishing grade school…

If you lived north of the James, odds are that, at some point, you attended **Chandler Junior High School.** Located on Brookland Park Boulevard, some of the areas most popular and populated neighborhoods fed into Chandler. Families that lived in Barton Heights, Highland Park, Bellevue, Sherwood Park, Ginter Park and numerous others sent their children to Chandler. After completing grades seven and eight, students went on to attend one of the two rival high schools: Thomas Jefferson or John Marshall.

Many marriages took place between grads of these rival high schools, but chances were they had met on the "common ground" of Chandler Junior High.

Department stores, movies, lunch or dinner...

South of the river and need a day of shopping? North of the river but want to take a drive to the area's first regional mall? **Cloverleaf Mall,** opened in 1972, was quite the destination for all the family's needs. Anchored by Sears, Thalhimer's, and J. C. Penney, Cloverleaf defined "suburban mall" for the central Virginia region. Picadilly Cafeteria, Spencer's Gifts, bookstores, clothing stores, jewelers and a two-screen cinema were just some of the destinations inside. Clearly, one could meander from open to close, breakfast to dinner, under the same roof at Cloverleaf Mall.

Additional malls took their toll on Cloverleaf. As the retail market expanded, people began to shop more in their own neighborhoods and the anchor tenants pulled out. Once that occurred, others followed suit and, by 2004, the Mall was a ghost town. But we had four decades of fun at Cloverleaf.

Robin Minton

Seafood? Special occasion?

Trying to plan a special night out for dinner? Looking for the right place to celebrate a special occasion such as a birthday, anniversary or retirement? In high school and want your date to think you knew what you were doing? If seafood was what you sought, there was only one choice – **The Flying Cloud.** One of Richmond's favorite restaurants located in the Westmoreland area, The Flying Cloud was among the places to see and be seen while you enjoyed a seafood meal in a nautical setting. Upscale dining without being uptight, it was the site for many after-church family dinners and celebrations for all generations. We all loved the Flying Cloud.

National restaurant chains opened seafood restaurants, expanded their menus, and ultimately, The Flying Cloud closed. But not until after having made many happy memories for us.

FOOD FAIR
OUR HIGHEST QUALITY
POTATO CHIPS
NET WT. 18 OZ. (1 LB. 2 OZ.) PAREVE

OUR EVERYDAY 95¢ LOW PRICE

FOOD FAIR
OUR HIGHEST QUALITY
POTATO CHIPS
NET WT. 18 OZ. (1 LB. 2 OZ.) PAREVE

OUR EVERYDAY 95¢ LOW PRICE

FAIR POTATO CHIPS
NET WT. 18 OZ. (1 LB. 2 OZ.) PAREVE

LOW PRICE

FAIR POTATO CHIPS
NET WT. 18 OZ. (1 LB. 2 OZ.) PAREVE

LOW PRICE

FAIR CHIPS
NET WT. 18

FOOD FAIR
OUR HIGHEST QUALITY
POTATO CHIPS
NET WT. 18 OZ. (1 LB. 2 OZ.) PAREVE

FOOD FAIR
OUR HIGHEST QUALITY
POTATO CHIPS
NET WT. 18 OZ. (1 LB. 2 OZ.) PAREVE

OUR EVERYDAY 95¢ LOW PRICE

FOOD FAIR
NET WT.

Just bread, eggs and milk? Or a full week's groceries?

Eastgate Mall, Azalea Mall, Henrico Plaza, Patterson Avenue. All had a store from the same chain. All were affiliated with Pantry Pride. What was the name of this "nonlocally-owned" supermarket? **Food Fair.** The stores became equally known for what was outside of the store as what was inside. They boasted the area's first electric-mat door openers. Many a child got in trouble for running in and out of the store to make the door open and shut. In front of each store sat "bucking bronco" animal rides. First for a dime and later for a quarter, kids could ride one of the plastic electric animals. Seems silly now, but we all loved them back then.

We all knew the manager and assistant manager of the closest Food Fair. Sitting up in the booth, they always waved. The stores were sold and ultimately closed long ago.

Tired of miniature golf and bowling?

High school groups. Families. Church groups. Teen birthday parties. Dates. Events of all shapes and sizes took place at **Golden Skate World** at Parham and Broad. Usually on a Friday night if it wasn't football season, or Saturday night if it was, our parents would drop us off with a pack of friends or a "date" and we felt like grown-ups out on the town. If you had a date, the hand-holding "Couple's Skate" was exhilarating. If you didn't have a date, it was time to grab a soda. And then there were the show-offs that could actually skate backwards to the rhythm of the music and the flash of the disco ball without falling. No matter how good you were, or how bad, it was fun skating with friends or family.

Hot dogs, skating, dating, hanging out – all part of growing up and the fun we had doing it.

Family or friends coming to town?
Business clients need a place to stay?

When an upscale hotel was needed and a suburban setting was desired, there was a single choice. Located in what was then considered Richmond's Far West End, Brookfield Business Park was developed at Interstate 64 and Broad Street. The cornerstone of that park was the **Hyatt House,** regarded by most as *the* place to stay, host events and enjoy fine dining. The four star restaurant, **Hugo's,** was the site for Richmond's most exquisite cuisine and hosted countless business dinners, celebrations, prom dates and holiday parties. There was no question where your special event needed to be held – the Hyatt House.

The hotel has gone through numerous names changes and owners over the years, but we will almost certainly know it as the Hyatt.

Burgers on the go? In a rush? Taking dinner home?

Whatever the reason, if we didn't have the time for a full service restaurant and had a hankering for a real burger, there was no question where we went: **Kelly's.** Known as the quickest burger place in town, Kelly's was once the home of "Jet-Fast Service" and the 15-cent burger (depending on your generation!). Whether Eastgate Mall, 5th and Broad or the Boulevard near Parker Field, the service was consistently fast and the food was always great. Parents, kids and friends – all the gang was happy. Kelly's was also well known for its "Fire Engine" television commercials. If a group of firemen could get their burgers on the way to a fire, surely it would work for all of us!

Kelly's fell by the wayside with the growth of the multi-national mega chains. Sure do miss the Kelly Burger, though.

That voice is everywhere...

Radio news reporter. Radio entertainer. Voice-over talent for commercials. Even the "Welcome to Richmond" greeting in Richmond International Airport. Who is that with the deep, firm, trustworthy voice? None other than **Lou Dean.** He served as master of ceremonies for various events all over Richmond. He covered everyday events as well as major happenings around the world. He could be heard on Richmond's beloved WRVA-1140 AM from 1957-2000. Call-in programs, overnight programs, news programs – throughout a five decade career, if WRVA did it, Lou Dean had a hand in it. After he left WRVA in 2000, he worked for Henrico County as a communications specialist until he took his much-deserved retirement in 2007.

In the present, when most radio shows are syndicated and recorded out of far-flung cities, it's nice to remember the days of information, entertainment and community brought to us through the voice of Lou Dean.

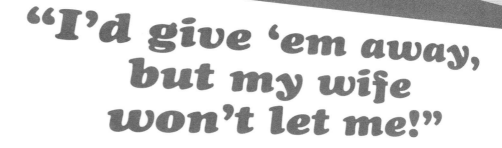

"I'd give 'em away, but my wife won't let me"

That slogan was seen and heard all over town – billboards, radio, television, newspapers – anywhere it could be used. What was the "em"? Used cars being sold by Richmond's own **Mad Man Dapper Dan.** The used car salesman, whose real name was Howard Hughes, was brilliant at marketing and making his pseudonym a household name. If you wanted a used car, you went to Mad Man Dapper Dan first.

Hughes was also known for his unique house on Cherokee Road, called the Moon House by Richmonders. Haig Jamgochian, the noted architect that designed Markel Corporation's "Reynold's Wrap" headquarters near Willow Lawn, also designed Hughes' home overlooking the James River. Sadly, the house was demolished by a developer. But the metallic aluminum foil building does still exist as an office building.

Craving the best dinner rolls in Richmond?

Buttery sweet potatoes? Chicken baked, fried, grilled and stuffed? We went to **Morton's Tea Room,** owned by Mrs. Julia Bell Morton. Mrs. Morton lived upstairs and had the Tea Room, a staple of southern hospitality, downstairs. She brewed her homemade iced tea with care and cooked her entrees, desserts and breads as if her own family members were eating each plateful of the delicious treats. Located at 2 East Franklin Street in downtown Richmond, the house was as elegant and gracious as its proprietor – a perfect match for a perfect meal.

Morton's closed in 1991 after 40 years of operation, and all of the regulars gathered for one final serving of dinner rolls – never to be duplicated as they had been prepared. The beautiful Tea Room is now an apartment building.

Bands? Packs of teens? Dancing?

Where was the one club or bar that was centrally located enough to draw from all over the area? Where did teens go in the 1970s and 80s to hear a band, have a beer, dance, hang out and look for dates? **Much More.** Located at the Boulevard and Broad St., Much More was a hang out and "much more" for the youth of those days. Bands were born. Couples met and broke up. Some teens drank their first legal beer there. Dancing was commonplace for the not-so-shy. And youth night was at least once a week so the 15, 16, and 17 year-old crowds could mingle and act as if they were already part of the "club set."

Clubs and bars tend to have a different stereotype now than those of 30 years ago. No metal detectors or security guards were needed back then.

Music? Albums?

We needed the latest pop or rock hits. We all had favorites. From classical to hard rock to disco to country. If you wanted to buy works from your favorite musicians, the first place to look was obvious: **Peaches Records and Tapes.** Any store with the words "records and tapes" is obsolete nowadays. Back then, we purchased singles on "45s" and full albums on "33s." Then came progress – the fabulous 8-track tapes. Technology then led us to the fascinating "cassette tape." Auto, home, record and tape players – Peaches had it all. There was also a Ticket-Master outlet located there to buy tickets for upcoming concerts. For all things musical, Peaches was *the* place.

CDs and MP3s are now the media of the day. But collectors still search far and wide for those albums, album covers, and cassettes.

Last minute or late night?

It's Christmas Eve and you've run out of wrapping paper and tape at midnight. Or worse, you still have presents to buy. A family member has fallen ill and you need to buy over-the-counter medicine or fill an urgent prescription in the middle of the night. Such things couldn't wait until morning when the stores open. So where did you go for last minute, late night shopping, drugs or sundries? **Peoples Drug** at Boulevard and Broad. Long before the mega-chains and their 24-hour shopping options, Peoples was the one location we could visit for what we needed, when we needed it. Who knows how many Christmases were saved with late-night runs to Peoples? And an infinite number of us got well a little sooner because we could get our prescriptions when we needed them, not 12 hours later.

The chain was ultimately bought by CVS, a company like many other national chains who routinely offer 24-hour services. Decades ago, however, we had Peoples. And we were glad for it.

Living south of the James – looking for a movie theater?

If you lived in South Richmond or Chesterfield County and wanted to see a "talkie," there were a couple of choices. If you were visiting friends and decided a movie was on the entertainment agenda, you went to the **Ponton Theater** or the **Venus Theater.** Both were located on Hull Street for your viewing pleasure. Mighty theater organs provided music and flickering projectors offered the moving pictures of the era. Known for showing the most up-to-date movies in the area, hundreds of patrons lined up weekly to see the latest releases. The Ponton is no more and the Venus Theater took on new life as a residential apartment building in recent years.

The Venus and Ponton had the same fate of so many of the area's single-screen cinemas as technology and larger theaters took over.

Before the days of buffet restaurants...

We liked going through a line and seeing our food as we ordered it. Meatloaf, chicken, potatoes, greens, chocolate cake and lime pudding. Comfort foods of our childhood. The occasional Salisbury steak would mix things up. Where did you go for this cafeteria-style of dining? **S & W Cafeteria** located at Willow Lawn Shopping Center or Southside Plaza. Faster than a full-service restaurant, but better than a fast food stop, S & W was known for serving up "home cooking" at affordable prices. Everyone liked it, and usually the whole family went to dine together. It wasn't unusual to see four generations on a family outing, each selecting what they wanted as they saw it.

Sure there was better food and better service. But sometimes, S & W was the only thing that would hit the spot.

If you lived in the East End, and needed prescriptions, breakfast, a milkshake, and toiletries….

Everyone in the East End knew to visit the **Sandston Pharmacy** on West Williamsburg Road. Bought from the previous owners in the 1940's, pharmacist and owner Tony Mehfoud turned the space into more than just a drugstore. It became a meeting spot, a social "hangout" for the Sandston crowd. Breakfast, lunch, milkshakes and limeades were all part of the café lifestyle at the Pharmacy. Mehfoud knew everyone in the area, and gave sage advice on healing, getting well, and just taking care of one another. Mehfoud served on the Henrico Board of Supervisors for decades and gave a great deal to the community through his public service. With a school named for him and a family following in the footsteps of service, the Mehfoud name and Sandston Pharmacy service won't soon be forgotten.

Mehdfoud's son and his wife run the store now. The prescription business was sold, but they are still known for their customer service and friendly approach, just like their beloved Tony would have wanted it.

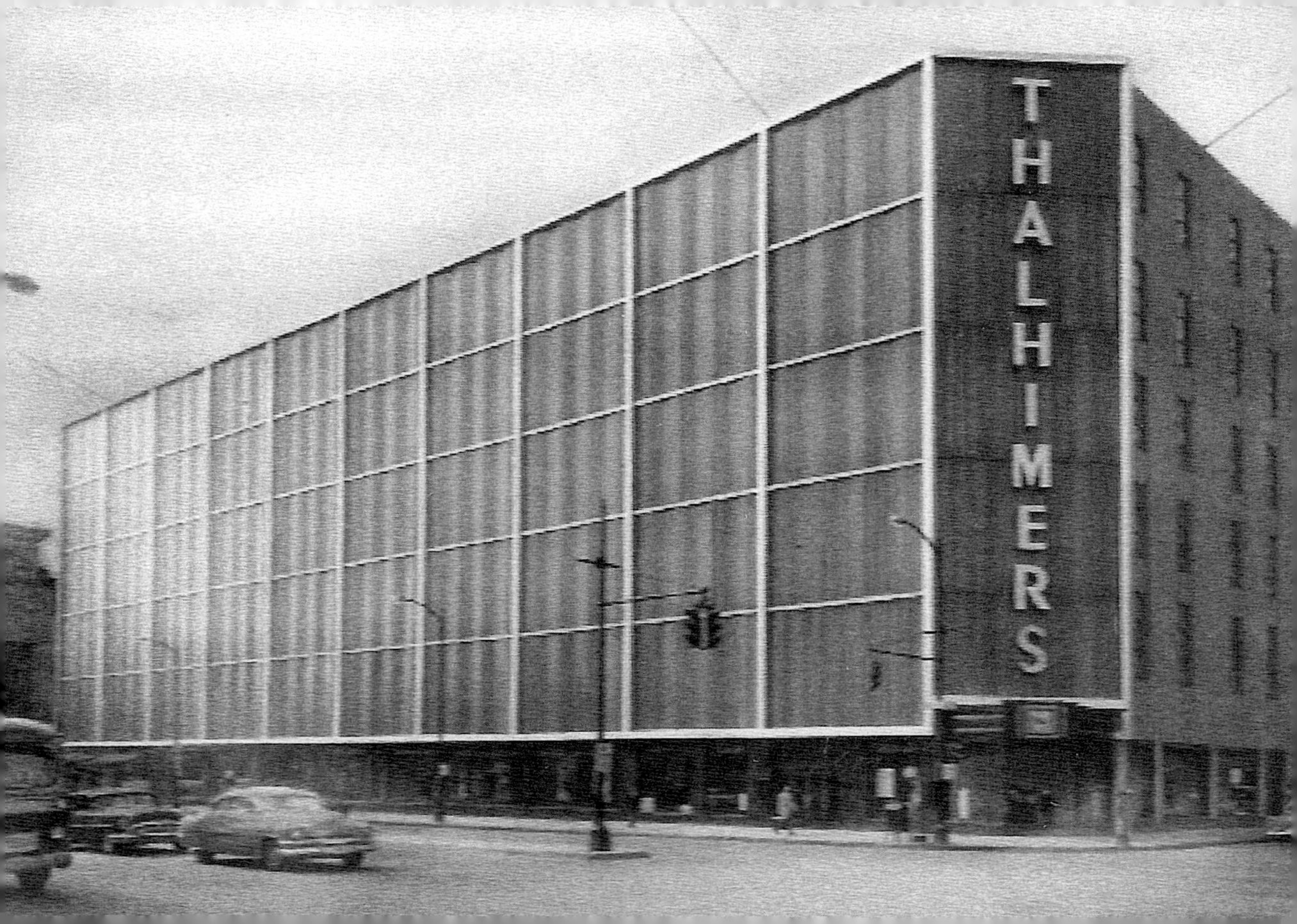
THALHIMERS

Time to shop...

Azalea. Downtown. Westmoreland. Cloverleaf Mall. And the list goes on. Looking for clothing, jewelry, house wares or the wedding registry? Need a baked good in the all-too-familiar black and white checked box? Lunch on the third floor of the Downtown store? Must be looking for one of our beloved **Thalhimers Department Stores.** In its heyday, Thalhimers had stores throughout the South. It was one of the premier places to shop, gather and enjoy. During the holidays, Snow Bear entertained thousands. To all of us living in the Richmond region, Thalhimers wasn't just a store. It was a destination, a culture, a part of us.

In 1990, the chain was sold to the May Company. By 1992, all of the remaining stores were merged into the brands of Hecht's and others owned by May. Thalhimers will always be a part of our heritage and our fond memories of shopping in Richmond.

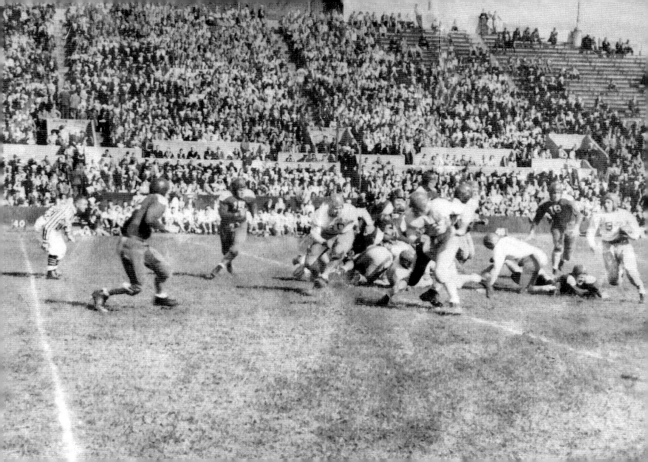

The much-anticipated game of the football season…

The Blue and White vs. the Red and White. It was a high school rivalry that was known around town for being fierce, not vindictive. The winner was the winner but the loser was not persecuted – they would get their chance on the gridiron next season. Obviously, the game being referred to was when **Thomas Jefferson High School** played **John Marshall High School.** The Jeffersonians played the Justices every year at Richmond City Stadium. Excitement built for weeks before. School colors weren't just worn the day of the game, but as part of everyday school clothes, on uniforms, in bows and ribbons – all to exhibit school spirit. It wasn't just a football game. It was an event that drew upwards of 25,000 people. It was a culture. It was the coming together of rivals in a competitive but respectful way.

All the city's eyes were on The Game. Not only for the winner, but also for the enjoyment of this rich and storied tradition.

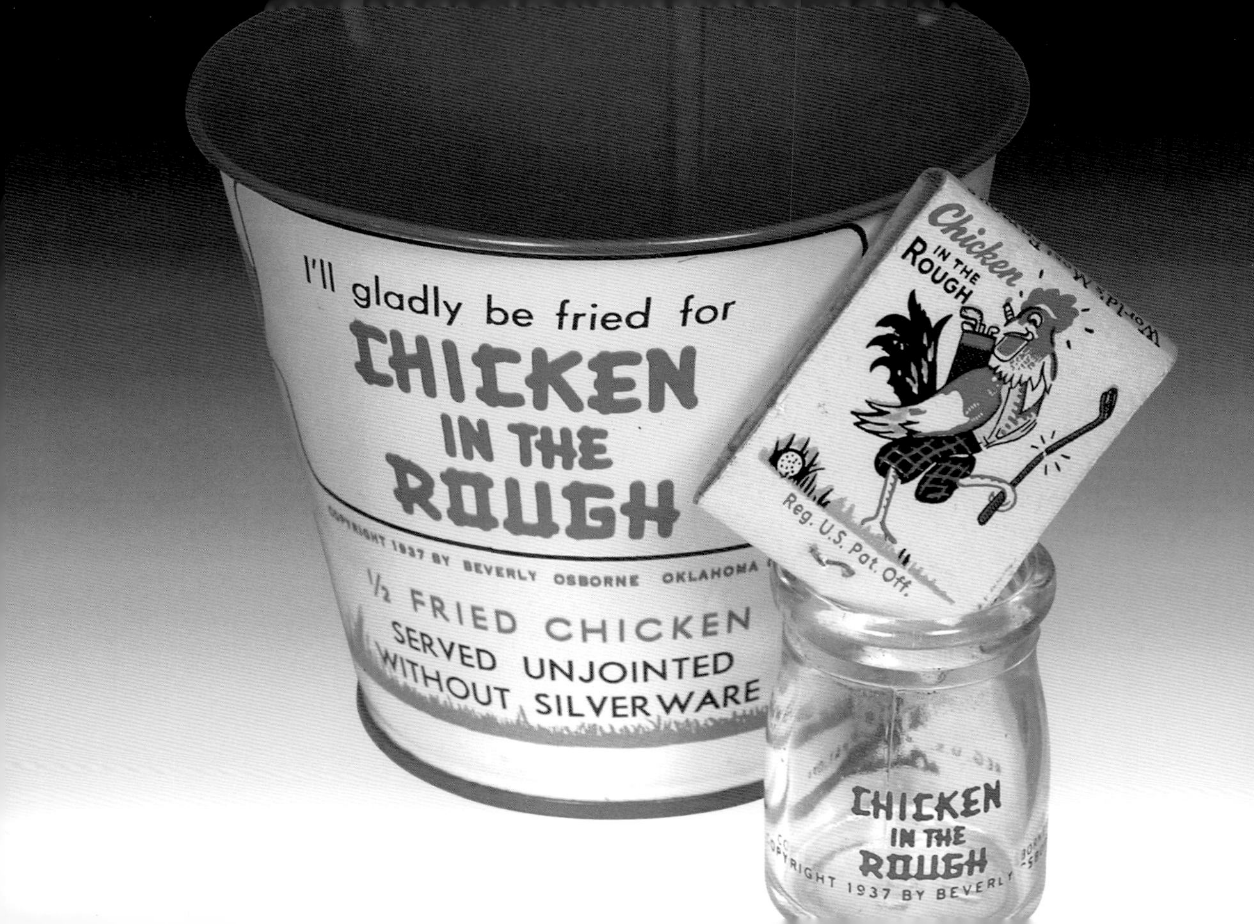

Landis Productions, LLC

The "Original" Chicken-in-the-Rough

Craving fried chicken? *Real* fried chicken? We went to the original home of the famous Chicken-in-the-Rough, **Wakefield Grill.** Located at 3124 West Broad Street, then considered Richmond's West End, countless baskets of chicken were served every day at lunch and dinner. Each meal even came complete with a bucket of water to wash the grease off your hands – napkins couldn't quite get the job done.

Sadly, Wakefield Grill was destroyed by fire in 1960. A year later, Lendy's opened Richmond's first Kentucky Fried Chicken at the same site. Though it was good, it never reached the level of taste and demand as Wakefield.

Wakefield Grill, 3124 West Broad, Richmond, Va.
PHONE 5-8987

PHONE 5-8987 CHICKEN IN THE ROUGH - STEAKS - SEA FOOD

Swimming in the suburbs?
A picnic and a dinner theatre at the same location?

What's that all about? Take the family for a picnic. Go swimming with your friends. Go out for a night on the town with dinner and a show at one of the area's few dinner theatres. But all at the same location? Located in Mechanicsville, **Westhaven Lake and the Haymarket Dinner Theatre** offered all of that. By day, a family "resort-type" atmosphere with a fully functional recreation area and lake. The building in front housed a dining room serving dinner and a stage showing the best in plays and musicals. This entertainment complex was located on Mechanicsville Turnpike, Route 360, just west of Battlefield Park Elementary School.

The lake is dry and full of weeds now, and the building has been turned over a dozen times with different restaurants, but it will always be referred to as "Westhaven" when native Richmonders pass by.

Dinner. Dancing. A teepee?

What's that strange combination? A place to go out to eat and dance. A motor court in the back. But then a log cabin with a teepee attached to it? Must be the **Wigwam Restaurant and Dance Hall.** Generations of Richmonders spent much of their nightlife at this destination spot, then considered almost "out of town." Seven miles north of Richmond and 3 miles south of Ashland, it was quite the drive in those days. But you could always count on great meals, big band music and a great evening of dancing with friends.

In the years after the popular nightspot closed, a flea market was opened at the Wigwam for bargain hunters to trap their prey. In 2002, the facility closed for good. Developers purchased the site and have announced that a mall will be developed. At the time of this writing, no dirt has been touched and the only things unearthed have been the fondest memories of the good times we had.

Do you need additional copies of "*Memory Lane, Richmond, VA – Vol. 1, 2 or 3*" to share with friends and family? Keep a sharp eye out for them at local retailers or visit www.kleosmagazine.com to order copies online.

Are you a big fan of a Richmond landmark we missed in Volume Three? Send a letter to KLEOS International, Inc., 8400 Meadowbridge Road, Mechanicsville, VA 23116 or visit www.kleosmagazine.com today to suggest entries for future volumes of "*Memory Lane.*"

Special thanks to: "At Last" at Antique Village, Bellevue Antiques, Joe Brooks, Val Emerson, Nancy Farrell, Frank Hargrove, Sr., Kathy Julian, David Landis, Joe Lipscombe, Steven Martinenza, Jimmy Mehfoud (Sandston Pharmacy), Robin and Dennis Minton, Sandra Nelson, Ouroboros at Antique Village, Roy Putze, Dolores Ross, Shirley Thomas, Whiting's Old Paper, George & Jeannette Williams and Janet Carlton Williams.